MUHAMMAD ALI

MUHAMMAD ALI

THE GREATEST

MATT DOEDEN

LERNER PUBLICATIONS ◆ MINNEAPOLIS

Lerner Publications Company
A division of Lerner Publishing Group, Inc.
241 First Avenue North
Minneapolis, MN USA 55401

For reading levels and more information, look up this title at www.lernerbooks.com.

The images in this book are used with the permission of: AP Photo/Rex Features, p. 2; AP Photo/Dan Grossi, p. 6; AP Photo, pp. 8 (left), 10, 16, 17, 18, 21, 27, 29, 32; © Bettmann/Getty Images, p. 8 (right); AP Photo/Reed Saxon, p. 9; © Jerry Cooke /Sports Illustrated/Getty Images, p. 12; Sergio Del Grande Mondadori Portfolio/Newscom, p. 13; AP Photo/Charles Dharapak, p. 20; © Everett Collection Historical/Alamy, p. 22; AP Photo/Joe Holloway Jr., p. 24; AP Photo/Eddie Adams, p. 26; AP Photo/Picture-Alliance, p. 30; Balkis Press/ABACAPRESS.COM/ Newscom, p. 34; © Stephen J. Boitano/LightRocket/Getty Images, p. 35; AP Photo/Michael Probst, p. 36; AP Photo/Jeff Roberson, p. 39.

Front cover: © Trevor Humphries/Getty Images.

Main body text set in Rotis Serif Std 55 Regular 13.5/17. Typeface provided by Adobe Systems.

Library of Congress Cataloging-in-Publication Data

Names: Doeden, Matt, author.
Title: Muhammad Ali : the greatest / by Matt Doeden.
Description: Minneapolis : Lerner Publications, [2017] | Series: Gateway Biographies | Includes
    bibliographical references, webography and index. | Audience: Ages: 9-14. | Audience:
    Grades: 4 to 6.
Identifiers: LCCN 2016030803 (print) | LCCN 2016038885 (ebook) | ISBN 9781512444315 (lb :
    alk. paper) | ISBN 9781512444322 (eb pdf)
Subjects: LCSH: Ali, Muhammad, 1942-2016—Juvenile literature. | Boxers (Sports)—United
    States—Biography—Juvenile literature. | Political activists—United States—Biography—Juvenile
    literature.
Classification: LCC GV1132.A4 D64 2017 (print) | LCC GV1132.A4 (ebook) | DDC 796.83092 [B]
    —dc23

LC record available at https://lccn.loc.gov/2016030803

Manufactured in the United States of America
1-42508-26186-8/19/2016

CONTENTS

Born Cassius Clay   9

Becoming the Greatest   11

Self-Promoter   14

New Name, New Outlook   15

A Different Kind of Fight   19

The Comeback   23

Rumbles and Thrillers   27

A Shadow of His Former Self   31

Life after Boxing   33

Remembering a Legend   37

Important Dates   40
Source Notes   42
Selected Bibliography   45
Further Reading   46
Index   48

Heavyweight fighter Cassius Clay spent many hours at City Parks Gym in New York in the 1960s.

Twelve men stood in a line in the Military Entrance Processing Station in Houston, Texas, on April 28, 1967. Among them was twenty-five-year-old Muhammad Ali, the world heavyweight champion in boxing and one of the most famous athletes in the world.

Ali looked on as the induction hearing got under way on that spring day. He and the others in the line were being asked to swear themselves into military service. The officer in charge of the hearing called out Ali's name. It was a moment months in the making.

Upon being drafted into—or required to join—the military in 1966, Ali had filed as a conscientious objector, or a person morally opposed to war. The officer overseeing his case had agreed that Ali's plea was sincere and had recommended Ali be cleared of military obligation. Usually that would have been enough. But Ali's wasn't just any case. He was a star and one publicly critical of the Vietnam War (1957–1975). His request had been refused.

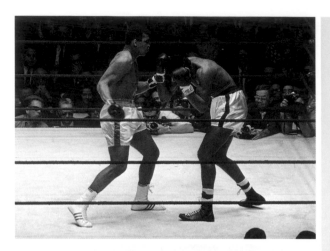

Muhammad Ali

Above: Muhammad Ali faces Ernie Terrell in the ring in 1967 before being stripped of his boxing title for draft evasion. *Right:* Ali signed this photo for a fan in Frankfurt, Germany, at the height of his career.

Now the situation was coming to a head. By stepping forward and swearing the oath, Ali would be turning his back on his own deeply held beliefs. By standing still, he would be branded a criminal.

Ali didn't move.

An officer led Ali from the room, explaining the consequences of refusal. Ali would be arrested. He risked a prison sentence. He would be stripped of his freedom and almost certainly his boxing title.

Ali returned to the induction hearing. He was being given a second chance to agree to military service. Again, his name was called. But again, Ali didn't budge. He was committed to refusing military assignment, regardless of the consequences.

"It is in the light of my consciousness as a Muslim minister and my own personal convictions that I take my stand in rejecting the call to be inducted," Ali explained in a statement. "I do so with the full realization of its implications. I have searched my conscience."

Two months later, Ali was formally charged with felony draft evasion. He was sentenced to five years in prison, fined $10,000, and stripped of his passport as well as his boxing titles. But the champ's fight was just beginning.

BORN CASSIUS CLAY

Cassius Marcellus Clay Jr. was born on January 17, 1942, in Louisville, Kentucky. He was named for his father, who in turn had been named for a famous but controversial

Ali delivers a friendly punch to his father, Cassius Clay Sr., during a news conference on January 4, 1980.

Even as a young teenager, Cassius Clay showed promise as a boxer. His training regimen included sparring with friends and running alongside the school bus.

abolitionist of the nineteenth century. Slavery was illegal in the 1940s, but its echoes remained. The South was segregated, with blacks and whites legally separated along color lines. Cassius grew up in a time and place where racism was rampant and many whites viewed blacks as second-class citizens.

Cassius's father worked as a painter. The family never had much money. Cassius couldn't afford the bus fare to school. So he'd run instead. He made it a race, trying to beat the bus to school.

Cassius's future began to take shape at the age of twelve, when his bicycle—a treasured gift from his father—was stolen. Cassius was furious. He told police officer Joe Martin that he intended to fight the thief. Martin, who was also a boxing coach, answered, "Well, you better learn how to fight before you start challenging people."

Martin began training Cassius, who thrived at the gym. "I was the first one in the gym, and the last to leave," he later said. "I trained six days a week."

Just six weeks later, Cassius—at eighty-nine pounds—had his first fight. His father watched from ringside as Cassius won a three-round split decision over an older, more experienced opponent. It was a modest victory for the boy who would one day become the greatest heavyweight of all time.

BECOMING THE GREATEST

Cassius threw himself into boxing, giving his all to the sport whenever he wasn't in school or sleeping. His goal was simple. He wanted to be the greatest—nothing less. Cassius woke up at four thirty in the morning to start training. As a teenager, he refused the temptations of drugs and alcohol. Those, he reasoned, would get in the way of his goal. He had little interest in other sports. He didn't like football, because he got hit in football. The same was rarely true in the ring. Cassius was just too quick on his feet. Nobody could touch him.

Cassius rose up the ranks quickly. As a teenager, he compiled an amateur record of 100–5 and won several major amateur titles along the way. He was one of the sport's rising stars. He won a spot on the 1960 US Olympic boxing team. Then afraid of airplanes, Cassius considered not making the trip to Rome, Italy. He did go despite his fears, and he fought in the light heavyweight division—one of the weight categories into which boxers are divided.

Cassius handily won his first three fights to advance to the final. There, he faced Poland's Zbigniew Pietrzykowski. Early on in the final, Cassius appeared off-balance, possibly because his opponent was left-handed—something Cassius wasn't used to. Entering the third and final round, Cassius knew that he was behind on the scorecards. So, needing to score big with the judges, he came out in full attack mode. Cassius peppered his opponent with punch after punch. As the final bell sounded, Pietrzykowski was on the ropes, battered and close to going down. The judges rewarded the effort. Cassius was the gold medalist.

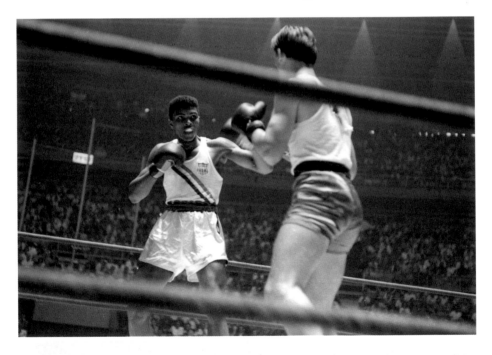

Cassius Clay goes up against Poland's Zbigniew Pietrzykowski in the 1960 Summer Olympics.

Famed American sprinter Wilma Rudolph also medaled for her country at the 1960 Olympic Games.

Cassius made his name with his fists. But it was his outgoing personality that propelled him to stardom. Even in the Olympic Village, among many of the world's greatest athletes, he was the center of attention. "Everybody wanted to see him," said US track star Wilma Rudolph. "Everybody wanted to be near him. Everybody wanted to talk to him. And he talked all the time."

Cassius's popularity wasn't limited to his fellow athletes. Back home in the United States, interest in the gold medalist was booming. Fans loved his brash style and confident manner. Upon returning from Rome, Cassius turned pro, beginning his quest for the heavyweight title. He was an artist in the ring, dancing and baiting his opponents into careless attacks, then blitzing them with jabs the moment they let down their guard. He often said his style was to float like a butterfly and sting like a bee—words he'd once heard someone else say and eventually adopted as his motto.

SELF-PROMOTER

Clay rarely missed an opportunity to promote himself. He proudly proclaimed his own greatness to anyone who would listen. In 1963 the twenty-one-year-old Clay even released a music album, *I Am the Greatest!* In it he taunted reigning champ Sonny Liston.

More important, Clay backed up his big talk. He quickly worked his way up the heavyweight ranks, finally earning a title fight against Liston in 1964.

Clay was a big underdog in the fight. Few experts thought he was ready to take on a seasoned bruiser like Liston. Even some in Clay's own camp discouraged him from taking the fight, fearing the bigger, more experienced Liston would pummel the youngster. Yet in the days leading up to the bout, Clay taunted his opponent. He dubbed Liston the big, ugly bear.

Liston *(right)* ducks low and weaves to escape a punch from Cassius Clay's cocked right fist during a fight in Miami Beach, Florida, on February 25, 1964.

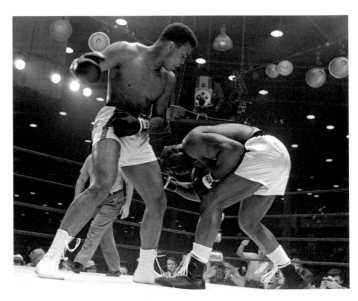

Liston didn't appreciate it. In the first round, the champ told Clay that he was going to kill him. Clay later confessed that it was the only time he'd ever been afraid in the ring.

Liston came out swinging. But Clay's speed allowed him to duck and dodge Liston's advances, making the champ look awkward and out of control. Clay pressed his advantage. He emerged from the fight victorious. Clay, at the age of twenty-two, was the world heavyweight champion—he had achieved his boyhood goal.

"I am the greatest!" Clay shouted. "I shook up the world!"

NEW NAME, NEW OUTLOOK

Clay's focus was on boxing. But he was also keenly aware of the larger issues around him. The 1960s were a time of political turmoil in the United States and abroad. The civil rights movement was in full swing, with black Americans demanding equal rights and treatment. It was a fight that appealed to Clay, who had always been deeply resentful of racism and America's legacy of slavery. By 1964 Clay's views on race had grown very strong, due in part to an association with a group called the Nation of Islam, or the Black Muslims.

Two major schools of thought drove the civil rights movement. The mainstream movement was one of passive resistance, led by Dr. Martin Luther King Jr. He promoted

Dr. Martin Luther King Jr. acknowledges the crowd at his historic "I Have a Dream" speech in Washington, DC, on August 28, 1963.

peaceful protest and civil disobedience, in the tradition of the well-known Indian leader Mahatma Gandhi.

Meanwhile, a second, smaller movement took the opposite approach. The Black Power movement, led by the Nation of Islam, took a militant stance on social reform. This movement endorsed violent uprising. It stood behind the idea that only forceful resistance would lead to true change when it came to civil rights.

For several years, Clay had been attending Nation of Islam meetings. "The first time I truly felt special in my life was when I walked into the Muslim temple in Miami," Clay explained. "I liked what I heard, and wanted to learn more. I had respect for Martin Luther King and other civil rights leaders, but I was taking a different road."

Over the years, Clay had gravitated more and more toward the Nation of Islam. Malcolm X, one of the movement's leaders and rising stars, had become his

personal mentor. Clay, raised a Baptist, was moved by
Malcolm X's teachings of Islam and black power. He had
converted to Islam and began referring to himself as
Cassius X, shedding what he referred to as his slave name.
After his defeat of Liston in 1964, he officially joined the
Nation of Islam and changed his name to Muhammad Ali.

"Cassius Clay is a slave name," Ali explained. "I didn't
choose it and I don't want it. I am Muhammad Ali, a free
name. It means beloved of God, and I insist people use it
when people speak to me."

Ali's name change and his affiliation with the Nation
of Islam changed the way many fans viewed him. The
group was highly controversial. Its leaders openly called
for violence against oppression, in direct contrast to

Ali *(right)* stands with
Malcolm X outside the
Trans-Lux Newsreel
Theater in New York
City on March 1, 1964.

King's teachings. Ali had won fans with his youthful excitement. That public view of him quickly faded away. Many saw him as a militant radical. Hate mail poured in. Ali's popularity dropped sharply, especially among white fans. The World Boxing Association, one of the sport's two major sanctioning bodies, stripped him of his title because of his membership in the Nation of Islam.

Meanwhile, shifting politics within the group left few feeling safe. Malcolm X was gunned down after falling out with its leader, Elijah Muhammad. And as Ali prepared to fight Sonny Liston in a May 1965 rematch, both men received threats against their lives.

The strange circumstances spilled into the ring. Ali knocked out Liston in the first round. Yet experts couldn't see anything that looked like a knockout blow. Rumors

World heavyweight champion Ali celebrates his victory as referee Joe Walcott counts out Sonny Liston on May 25, 1965.

swirled about a phantom punch. Many thought that Liston had taken a dive on purpose. Some suggested that Liston had lost to pay off gambling debts. But later evidence suggests that Liston did it because he feared for his life and the lives of his family. Regardless of the truth, the fight clearly appeared to be dirty. It left a stain on the reputations of all involved.

Two years later, Ali defended his title against Ernie Terrell. The two were bitter rivals. Terrell angered Ali by calling him Clay, the name he had abandoned. Terrell claimed that he'd done so merely by force of habit, having known Ali before his name change. Yet Ali raged at the perceived insult. He promised to torture Terrell in the ring. And he did. Ali dominated the fight. But he toyed with Terrell. He prolonged the fight to fifteen rounds, even though it appeared that he could have easily ended it much earlier. Ali was determined not just to win but to inflict maximum damage on Terrell for his insults. Experts called it one of the dirtiest fights in boxing history. Some wondered whether Ali's behavior was consistent with a man who was claiming to be a pacifist. But for Ali, pacifism meant he was against fighting in the Vietnam War—not against unleashing punches in the ring.

A DIFFERENT KIND OF FIGHT

Ali's victory over Terrell allowed him to focus on another issue—his military draft status. The Vietnam War was in

THE LOUISVILLE LIP

Whether he was trash-talking his opponent or promoting himself, Ali had a way with words. He loved speaking in rhymes and verse. In 1960 the Louisville Lip, as the press called Ali, spoke of his quest for Olympic gold.

> To make America the greatest is my goal,
> so I beat the Russian and I beat the Pole.
> And for the USA won the medal of gold.
> The Greeks said you're better than the Cassius of old.

Celebrated poet Maya Angelou was among Ali's fans. "It wasn't *only* what he said and it wasn't *only* how he said it," Angelou explained. "It was both of those things, and maybe there was a third thing in it, the spirit of Muhammad Ali."

Renowned author Maya Angelou, who died in 2014 at the age of eighty-six, was an admirer of Ali and his way with words.

full swing. In 1964 Ali had been granted exempt status to the military draft because of poor scores on intelligence tests. That status had changed in 1966 when the military adopted new standards. Ali was no longer exempt. That meant that he was compelled to enlist.

Ali had refused. "I ain't got no quarrel with them Viet Cong," he'd explained, referring to the North Vietnamese against whom US forces were fighting. He added that he would go to war only if Allah (the name of God in Islam) ordered it.

These were not popular opinions. The Vietnam War still had widespread support in the United States. Those viewed as draft dodgers were often seen as cowards or unpatriotic. Many

Ali appears at a news conference in Louisville, Kentucky, on April 20, 1967, to say he will not take part in miltary service of any nature.

Supporters of Ali cheer on a man burning a draft card in Houston, Texas.

despised Ali for his refusal. But others—especially in the black community—praised him. Ali helped bring attention to the fact that the majority of those drafted were from the lower and middle classes.

Ali tried—and failed—to achieve conscientious objector status. And so when he formally refused military assignment at his induction hearing in 1967, he was charged with felony draft evasion. He was stripped of his title, barred from boxing, and faced a five-year prison term.

It was a dark time for Ali. A friend suggested that the champ flee to Canada to avoid criminal prosecution. Ali was furious at the idea. "America is my home. Do you think I would let somebody chase me out of my home?" Ali demanded. "Nobody is going to chase me out of my birthplace. If they say I have to go to jail, then I will. But I'm not gonna run away, and you should know it."

Ali, right in the prime of his career, was banned from the ring. So he put his focus into a different kind of fight—a legal appeal. It lasted more than three years. During that time, Ali served as a guest lecturer on college campuses and even appeared in a Broadway musical. The US Supreme Court ultimately sided with Ali. In 1971 the court unanimously overturned his conviction.

THE COMEBACK

Ali didn't have to wait for the Supreme Court ruling to return to the ring, however. By 1970 public opinion had turned sharply against the war. Many viewed Ali's refusal to join the military in a new light. The boxing ban had been lifted, and Ali was allowed to return to the ring to pursue the title that had been taken from him.

Ali returned a changed man and a changed fighter. At the age of twenty-nine, he was bigger and stronger than before, but that size came at the expense of his trademark speed and agility. He could no longer rely on his quick feet to duck, dodge, and dance around opponents. Ali had become less like a butterfly but more like a bee.

Ali was forced to adopt a new style, going toe-to-toe with opponents. One boxing expert later commented that the two greatest heavyweights in history were Cassius Clay and Muhammad Ali, so different was Ali's style when he stepped back into the ring in 1970.

Ali's first fight was in Atlanta, Georgia. There, in the heart of the Deep South, where segregation was making its last stand, he took on a white fighter, Jerry Quarry. Ali understood the social importance of the fight, set against the backdrop of the ongoing civil rights movement. In the days leading up to the fight, he was unusually restrained. He saved his message for the ring, where he left no doubt. Ali dominated Quarry, knocking him out in three rounds.

Ali delivers a hard right to Jerry Quarry on October 26, 1970, in a fight in Atlanta, Georgia.

The Quarry fight was really little more than a tune-up, as was his next fight, a hard-fought victory over Oscar Bonavena. Ali's real focus was on Joe Frazier, the man who had risen up and claimed the heavyweight crown during Ali's ban. The fighter known as Smokin' Joe was a fearsome foe. Frazier was a pure puncher. Ali, lacking the elusiveness of his youth, was about to face a new test. Could he take a punch?

The two biggest names in boxing took the ring in New York City's Madison Square Garden on March 8, 1971. It was dubbed the Match of the Century. And Ali was back to his old tricks, verbally assaulting Frazier in the weeks leading up to the match. "Joe Frazier is too ugly to be champ," Ali teased. "Joe Frazier is too dumb to be champ." And the insults got worse from there.

Ali claimed that his trash talking was just showmanship. But many others felt it was over the top and mean-spirited. Decades passed before Frazier finally forgave Ali for his harsh words.

Ali's taunting continued in the early rounds of the fight. Ali lifted his arms, inviting Frazier to hit his body. Then Ali would shake his head no to show that he wasn't harmed.

The fight dragged on, with Ali doing his best to match Frazier punch for punch. However, it was a style far better suited to Frazier than to Ali. Ali managed to survive all fifteen rounds, but the judges' decision was easy—Frazier was the clear winner. Ali, having suffered the first loss of his pro career, was gracious in defeat. "Joe earned it," he conceded.

JOE FRAZIER

Ali's greatest rival was Joe Frazier. Frazier rose to fame at the 1964 Olympics, where he won gold despite a broken thumb. With Ali banned in the late 1960s, Frazier filled the role as the world's most fearsome heavyweight.

Frazier stood just under six feet tall, on the small side for a heavyweight. But he was a powerful puncher who overcame his smaller stature by using a dizzying bob-and-weave defense. He earned the heavyweight title in 1970 and successfully defended it against Ali in 1971.

Frazier finished his pro career with a record of 37–4–1. He died of liver cancer in 2011.

Ali *(left)* and Joe Frazier go head-to-head in New York's Madison Square Garden on March 8, 1971.

RUMBLES AND THRILLERS

Ali had lost, but his comeback was just beginning. Ali was determined to regain what had been taken from him—the heavyweight championship and his status as "the greatest."

As Ali's conditioning improved, so did his results. Ali won each of his next ten fights, pushing his career mark to 41–1. Then, in 1973, Ali lost to Ken Norton, who broke Ali's jaw during their bout. Yet Ali pressed on, beating Norton in a rematch just six months later. Still, his gaze remained fixed on the heavyweight title.

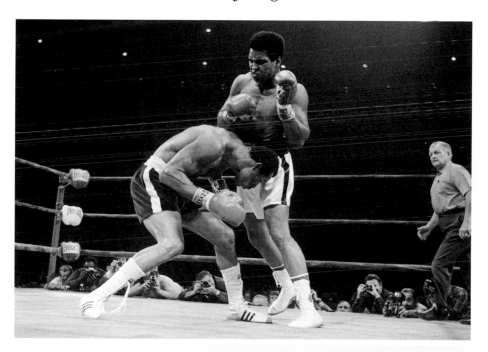

Ken Norton goes into a crouch to get away from Ali's attack in the first round of their twelve-round fight in Inglewood, California, on September 10, 1973.

A new man stood between Ali and his goal—George Foreman, who had taken the title from Frazier. But first came a rematch with Frazier in New York City. This time, Ali was in better condition. He'd learned from their first fight and was better able to exchange punches with Frazier. It was a tightly contested fight, but the judges awarded the victory to Ali.

That set the stage for a Foreman fight. Foreman was a giant of a fighter who overwhelmed opponents with pure power. Ali demanded $5 million for the fight. It was then an amazing sum. But the president of the central African nation of Zaire put up the money, believing that hosting such an event would be good for the nation. And so it was on. Ali traveled to Africa to prepare for the Rumble in the Jungle.

For Ali the trip was about more than just Foreman. Africa—the home of his ancestors—was a magical place to him. Ali absorbed the culture of Zaire. He loved being out among the people in the poor areas, and the people of Zaire embraced him, chanting his name everywhere he went. "To see the looks on people's faces when they saw him, the love, the power he had over them, it was spine-tingling," said Ferdie Pacheco, Ali's fight doctor.

The fight, held on October 30, 1974, more than lived up to its billing. It was held under a moonlit sky in the middle of the night so that it could be broadcast in prime time back in the United States. Ali's plan entering the fight had been to dance and move, making the bigger Foreman chase him around the ring. He hoped that

Ali *(left)* goes up against George Foreman in Zaire, Africa, on October 30, 1974.

Foreman would tire quickly. But after a single round, Ali felt sluggish. He abandoned the strategy.

Instead, Ali shocked his trainers by using a new strategy—the rope-a-dope. He hung back against the ropes and let Foreman pummel him with punches. It seemed like a crazy tactic. But Ali reasoned that he could conserve energy, while Foreman wore himself out punching. And he was right. By the eighth round, Foreman was running out of gas. Ali pounced, stinging the bigger man with a series of punches and sending him to the mat. Foreman managed to get up before he was counted out, but he couldn't go on. It was over. At the age of thirty-three, Muhammad Ali was once again the champ. Three hours later, he was performing magic tricks for the children of Zaire.

With his comeback complete, Ali had again staked his claim as the greatest. And once again, the public embraced him. Ali wasn't about to let the spotlight slip away. He agreed to another bout with his rival, Joe Frazier. The men met in the Philippines in October 1975.

The Thrilla in Manila was their third and final match.

Ali *(left)* delivers a blow to Joe Frazier during their 1975 fight in the Philippines.

It would prove the most demanding of Ali's career. The two legends went toe-to-toe in stifling heat of more than one hundred degrees. It was a sweat-drenched slugfest. Both men dished out—and absorbed—brutal poundings. In the early rounds, Frazier was the aggressor. He chased Ali around the ring, stinging him with body shots. But in the later rounds, Frazier began to tire. Ali became the aggressor. He pummeled Frazier's head with punches. By the fourteenth round, Frazier's face was a mess. His eyes were swollen shut. Frazier's trainers could see that he couldn't continue. They threw a towel into the ring—a signal in boxing that a fighter has had enough.

Ali was again the victor. But the fight had taken a heavy toll on the champ. "We went to Manila as champions, Joe and me," Ali later said. "And we came back as old men."

The physical punishment left Ali drained. "The ship stops here. My God, what that man did to me," Ali said, looking out over the Manila coastline. "No more oceans. Nothin' in boxin' for me no more."

Ali, at thirty-three years old, seemed to sense that it was time to walk away from boxing. But the champ didn't listen to his own instincts. Ali fought on.

A SHADOW OF HIS FORMER SELF

Ali held his title for three more years. But many of his fights during this period were long slugfests. The toll

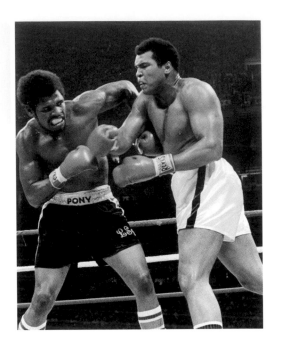

Ali *(right)* and Leon Spinks exchange punches during their World Boxing Association heavyweight title bout on September 16, 1978.

on Ali's body and mind mounted as the rounds and punches piled up. Finally, in February 1978, up-and-coming heavyweight Leon Spinks beat Ali to claim the heavyweight title. Surprisingly, seven months later, the thirty-six-year-old Ali bounced back to beat Spinks and reclaim his title. In doing so, he became the first heavyweight ever to win it on three separate occasions.

That seemed to be enough for Ali. Any doubts about his lifelong quest to become the greatest had been long since erased. In June 1979, Ali announced his retirement.

Ali was restless in retirement. He tried his hand at acting. He briefly served as a US diplomat, traveling to Africa to raise support for the US boycott of the 1980 Olympic Games (a boycott the United States initiated to protest the invasion of Afghanistan by the Soviet Union, a former nation made up of fifteen republics). None of it satisfied him. And so he decided on a comeback.

Many cautioned Ali. Even his mother begged him not to return. A prefight medical examination cleared him to fight but revealed some real concerns about Ali's health.

The report noted Ali's struggles with speech as well as failure to complete some basic tests of coordination. None of it swayed Ali. He was determined to return to the ring.

The comeback was a disaster. In October 1980, the thirty-nine-year-old Ali took on the new champ, Larry Holmes. Ali was a shadow of his former self. Holmes—who had grown up idolizing Ali—was in such control that he eased off Ali in the later rounds, not wanting to hurt or humiliate the man he admired.

"It is sad to see this," said broadcasting legend Howard Cosell during the match. "This must be stopped. . . . [Ali's] hands are no longer busy, his feet no longer swift."

For boxing fans, it was tragic to see Ali in such a state. Holmes, in victory, was in tears after seeing his hero so badly beaten. And yet, despite all of this, Ali still wouldn't hang up the gloves. He didn't want that to be his swan song. So Ali fought one more time, against Trevor Berbick. It was a ten-round defeat, by unanimous decision. Then it was clear even to Ali. His boxing career was over. He didn't have any more comebacks left.

LIFE AFTER BOXING

With his final defeat, it was time for Ali to turn to a new chapter in his life. "Boxing was the dressing room," he said shortly before his retirement, "a preliminary to the big fight for humanity, racial justice, freedom, and human rights."

Ali's focus turned to spirituality and helping others. His introduction to Islam through the Nation of Islam had been, in part, political. But by the mid-1970s, he'd converted to Sunni Islam, which brought with it a more spiritual outlook. Ali cited a 1972 pilgrimage to the holy city of Mecca for his new perspective. "I have never before seen sincere and true brotherhood practiced by all colors together, irrespective of their color," he explained.

The Great Mosque in Mecca, Saudi Arabia, in the final days of Ramadan in July 2016

Ali's faith would be tested in 1984. Friends and family noticed his health declining. His movements were less fluid. His speech was slow and slurred. Doctors diagnosed him with Parkinson's syndrome (later changing the diagnosis to Parkinson's disease). The disease, which often comes as a result of head trauma, was slowly robbing Ali of his abilities to move and speak.

Ali poses for a photo in 2009. Parkinson's disease had severely restricted the former boxing champ's movements by this time.

Yet Ali's mind remained sharp. He continued to embrace life and advocate for the less fortunate, both in the United States and abroad. He even returned to the ring, in a manner of speaking, serving as a guest referee in pro wrestling's *WrestleMania* in 1985. Ali's playful personality never faded. He loved to joke around with his friends and spend time with children, shadow boxing and doing magic tricks.

In the early 1990s, Ali traveled to Iraq, where fourteen US hostages were being held. Ali met with Iraqi dictator Saddam Hussein to appeal for the lives of the hostages.

And he succeeded. The hostages were freed. He would serve, on and off, as a diplomat for the United States throughout the rest of his life.

Ali was honored at the Olympic Games in Atlanta in 1996. To thunderous applause, he lit the Olympic torch at the opening ceremonies. By then his movements were slow and filled with tremor. His speech was labored. Yet he continued to soak in the attention. And he never lost

Ali was met with passionate cheering and worldwide acclaim when he lit the Olympic torch in Atlanta, Georgia, in 1996.

the self-confidence that had marked his career, continuing to refer to himself as the greatest. In 2001 the film *Ali* was released, to critical acclaim. It starred Will Smith in the role of Ali.

After terrorists from an Islamic extremist group launched attacks in New York City and near Washington, DC, on September 11, 2001, Ali was outspoken in defending Islam. Ten days after the attacks, he appeared on national television. Ali asked people not to identify Islam with terrorism. "I wouldn't be here representing Islam if it was really like the terrorists made it look," he explained in slow speech. "Islam is peace, against killing, murder, and the terrorists, and the people doing it in the name of Islam are wrong."

Ali's attention turned toward the disease that afflicted him. He teamed with popular actor Michael J. Fox to spearhead a campaign seeking to cure Parkinson's. The pair appeared before the US Congress in 2002 to appeal for help. Research into the causes of the disease and its cure are ongoing.

REMEMBERING A LEGEND

Ali's health continued to decline. Later, he was confined to a wheelchair. He could barely speak. On June 2, 2016, Ali was hospitalized with a respiratory illness. At first, his condition was listed as fair. But the champ never recovered. He died on June 3 at the age of seventy-four.

CHIP OFF THE OLD BLOCK

Ali married four times. He had nine children, two sons and seven daughters. Among them was daughter Laila, who chose to follow in her father's footsteps. Laila started boxing at the age of eighteen, despite her father's objections. Ali knew firsthand the dangers that went with taking repeated blows to the head.

Laila made her pro debut in 1999, at the age of twenty-one. She proved worthy of her father's legacy. Over eight years, she went 24–0, with twenty-one knockouts. She earned titles in the light middleweight and super middleweight divisions before retiring in 2007.

Ali's death made international headlines. Around the world, people mourned his loss and remembered his life and achievements. He was remembered not only as one of the great athletes of his time but as an icon of both political and popular culture.

Ali had expressed a wish that his memorial service be open to all. And so it was, with more than fifteen thousand people attending. It was a celebration of Ali, his life, and his accomplishments. People of all backgrounds and faiths came together to pay their respects. They included former president Bill Clinton, actors Billy Crystal and Will Smith, activist Jesse Jackson, and boxer Sugar Ray Leonard.

Crystal, a longtime friend of Ali, gave a heartfelt eulogy. "[Ali] was a tremendous bolt of lightning created by Mother Nature out of thin air, a fantastic combination of power and beauty. . . . Ali forced us to take a look at ourselves, this brash young man who thrilled us, angered us, confused and challenged us, ultimately became a silent messenger of peace, who taught us that life is best when you build bridges between people, not walls."

Muhammad Ali's funeral procession passes as onlookers line the street on June 10, 2016, in Louisville, Kentucky.

IMPORTANT DATES

1942 Muhammad Ali is born on January 17 in Louisville, Kentucky, as Cassius Clay.

1954 He takes up boxing after his bike is stolen.

1960 He earns Olympic gold in Rome, Italy. He wins his first pro fight in October.

1964 He beats Sonny Liston to claim the heavyweight crown. He formally joins the Nation of Islam and changes his name to Muhammad Ali.

1967 He refuses to enter military service and is convicted of felony draft evasion.

1970 After a three-year ban, Ali returns to the ring.

1971 The US Supreme Court overturns Ali's conviction for draft evasion. Ali loses his first fight against Joe Frazier.

1972 He takes a pilgrimage to the holy city of Mecca, which leads him to convert to Sunni Islam.

1974 He defeats George Foreman in the Rumble in the Jungle in Zaire to reclaim his heavyweight title.

1975	He beats Frazier in the Thrilla in Manila, which many regard as the peak of his boxing career.
1978	He claims the heavyweight title a record third time by beating Leon Spinks.
1981	He enters the ring a final time in a loss to Trevor Berbick.
1984	He is diagnosed with Parkinson's.
1996	He lights the torch at the Olympic Games Opening Ceremony in Atlanta, Georgia.
2016	He dies on June 3 at the age of seventy-four.

SOURCE NOTES

9 "From the Archive, 29 April 1967: Muhammad Ali Refuses to Fight in Vietnam War," *Guardian* (US ed.), April 29, 1967, http://www.theguardian.com/theguardian/2013/apr/29/muhammad-ali-refuses-to-fight-in-vietnam-war-1967.

10 Howard L. Bingham and Max Wallace, *Muhammad Ali's Greatest Fight: Cassius Clay vs. the United States of America* (Lanham, MD: M. Evans, 2000), 19.

10 John Micklos Jr., *Muhammad Ali: "I Am the Greatest"* (Berkeley Heights, NJ: Enslow, 2010), 16.

13 David Remnick, *King of the World: Muhammad Ali and the Rise of an American Hero* (New York: Vintage Books, 1998), 102.

15 Muhammad Ali and Hana Yasmeen Ali, *The Soul of a Butterfly: Reflections on Life's Journey* (New York: Simon & Schuster, 2004), 37.

16 Sean Gregory, "Why Muhammad Ali Matters to Everyone," *Time*, June 4, 2016, http://time.com/3646214/muhammad-ali-dead-obituary.

17 Suzette Gutierrez Cachila, "Why Did Muhammad Ali Convert to Islam?," *Christian Times*, June 9, 2016, http://christiantimes.com/article/why-did-muhammad-ali-convert-to-islam/56809.htm.

20 "Muhammed Ali—in His Own Words," *BBC*, June 4, 2016, http://www.bbc.com/sport/boxing/16146367.

20 Henry Louis Gates Jr., "Muhammad Ali, the Political Poet," *New York Times*, June 9, 2016, http://www.nytimes.com/2016/06/09/opinion/muhammad-ali-the-political-poet.html?_r=0.

21 Stefan Fatsis, "'No Viet Cong Ever Called Me Nigger': The Story behind the Famous Quote That Muhammad Ali Probably Never

Said," *Slate*, June 8, 2016, http://www.slate.com/articles/sports /sports_nut/2016/06/did_muhammad_ali_ever_say_no_viet_ cong_ever_called_me_nigger.html.

22 Jerry Izenberg, "Muhammad Ali: Why They Called Him 'The Greatest' and Why I Called Him My Friend," *NJ.com*, June 4, 2016, http://www.nj.com/sports/index.ssf/2016/06/former_ heavyweight_champ_muhammad_ali_dies_the_gre.html.

25 William Nack, "The Fight's Over, Joe," *SI.com*, September 30, 1996, http://www.si.com/vault/1996/09/30/208924/muhammad -ali-joe-frazier-war-of-words.

25 Gregory, "Why Muhammad Ali Matters."

28 Ibid.

31 Mark Kram, *Ghosts of Manila: The Fateful Blood Feud between Muhammad Ali and Joe Frazier* (New York: HarperCollins, 2002), 1.

31 Gregory, "Why Muhammad Ali Matters."

33 Ibid.

33 Dave Brady, "Ali Remains Elusive on Retirement," *Washington Post*, September 17, 1978, https://www.washingtonpost.com /archive/sports/1978/09/17/ali-remains-evasive-on-retirement /ad124c39-02c2-4298-94d9-832db966d0f4/.

34 Tim Stanley, "Muhammad Ali Was an American Idol and a Muslim. Read His Words on Islam," *Telegraph* (London), June 4, 2016, http://www.telegraph.co.uk/opinion/2016/06/04 /muhammad-ali-was-an-american-idol-and-a-muslim-read-his -words-on.

37 Gregory, "Why Muhammad Ali Matters."

39 "In Their Own Words: Eulogies for Muhammad Ali," *New York Times*, June 10, 2016, http://www.nytimes.com/2016/06/11 /sports/lonnie-billy-crystal-bill-clinton-eulogies-for-muhammad -ali.html?_r=0.

SELECTED BIBLIOGRAPHY

Ali, Muhammad. *The Greatest: My Own Story*. Nashville: Graymalkin, 1975.

Ali, Muhammad, and Hana Yasmeen Ali. *The Soul of a Butterfly: Reflections on Life's Journey*. New York: Simon & Schuster, 2004.

Bingham, Howard L., and Max Wallace. *Muhammad Ali's Greatest Fight: Cassius Clay vs. the United States of America*. Lanham, MD: M. Evans, 2000.

Edmunds, Anthony O. *Muhammad Ali: A Biography*. Westport, CT: Greenwood, 2006.

"From the Archive, 29 April 1967: Muhammad Ali Refuses to Fight in Vietnam War." *Guardian* (US ed.), April 29, 1967. http://www .theguardian.com/theguardian/2013/apr/29/muhammad-ali-refuses -to-fight-in-vietnam-war-1967.

Gregory, Sean. "Why Muhammad Ali Matters to Everyone." *Time*, June 4, 2016. http://time.com/3646214/muhammad-ali-dead-obituary.

Kram, Mark. *Ghosts of Manila: The Fateful Blood Feud between Muhammad Ali and Joe Frazier*. New York: HarperCollins, 2002.

Micklos, John, Jr. *Muhammad Ali: "I Am the Greatest."* Berkeley Heights, NJ: Enslow, 2010.

Remnick, David. *King of the World: Muhammad Ali and the Rise of an American Hero*. New York: Vintage Books, 1998.

FURTHER READING

BOOKS

Denenberg, Barry. *Ali: An American Champion.* New York: Simon &
    Schuster Books for Young Readers, 2014. Denenberg traces Ali's life
    and career alongside events that changed the United States, showing
    his impact on the political and popular culture of his country and
    the world.

Down, Susan Brophy. *Muhammad Ali: The Greatest.* New York: Crabtree,
    2013. Learn more about Ali's life, from his upbringing in Kentucky
    to his reigns as the heavyweight champion.

Hanzie, Christopher. *Punch: All about Boxing.* Cambridge: Cambridge
    University Press, 2014. Read more about the history, rules, and
    strategies of boxing as well as the sport's all-time greats.

WEBSITES

American Parkinson Disease Association—What Is Parkinson's Disease?
http://www.apdaparkinson.org/parkinsons-disease/understanding
-the-basics
Learn more about the neurological disease that affected Muhammad
Ali, including its causes, treatments, and research into the disease.

iWonder—Muhammad Ali: The Ultimate Fighter
http://www.bbc.co.uk/timelines/zy3hycw
View an interactive timeline of Muhammad Ali's life and boxing
career with links to related subjects and resources.

Muhammad Ali Center
http://www.alicenter.org
The Muhammad Ali Center is an event center and museum
devoted to the principles of Muhammad Ali. Their website includes
information on exhibits and programs.

INDEX

Ali, 37
Ali, Laila, 38
Angelou, Maya, 20

Berbick, Trevor, 33
Black Power movement, 16–17
Bonavena, Oscar, 25

civil rights movement, 15–16, 24
Cosell, Howard, 33
Crystal, Billy, 38–39

Foreman, George, 28–29
Fox, Michael J., 37
Frazier, Joe, 25, 26, 28, 30–31

Holmes, Larry, 33

I Am the Greatest!, 14

King, Martin Luther, Jr., 15–16, 18

Liston, Sonny, 14–15, 17, 18–19

Malcolm X, 16–18
Martin, Joe, 10
Match of the Century, 25
Mecca, 34

Nation of Islam, 15–18, 34
Norton, Ken, 27

Olympic Games, 11, 13, 20, 26, 32, 36

Parkinson's disease, 35, 37
Pietrzykowski, Zbigniew, 12

Quarry, Jerry, 24–25

rope-a-dope, 29
Rudolph, Wilma, 13
Rumble in the Jungle, 28

Saddam Hussein, 35
Spinks, Leon, 32

Terrell, Ernie, 8, 19
Thrilla in Manila, 30

Vietnam War, 7, 19, 21, 23

WrestleMania, 35